MW00696356

Best Wedding Meditations

An Anthology

CSS Publishing Company, Inc., Lima, Ohio

BEST WEDDING MEDITATIONS

Revised Edition 1997

Copyright © 1972 by
CSS Publishing Company, Inc.
Lima, Ohio
Second Printing 1976

Library of Congress Cataloging-in-Publication Data

Best wedding meditations : an anthology.
    p.   cm.
Includes bibliographical references.
ISBN 0-7880-0871-4 (pbk.)
1. Wedding sermons. 2. Marriage service.
BV4278.B47   1997
252'.1—dc20

96-38675
CIP

This book is available in the following formats, listed by ISBN:
    0-7880-0871-4   Book
    0-7880-1007-1   IBM 3 1/2
    0-7880-1006-9   Mac
    0-7880-1008-5   Sermon Prep

PRINTED IN U.S.A.

Table Of Contents

Preface

The marriage service, along with birth and death, remains as one of the high points in the personal lives and celebrations of our church members. And it is the greatest privilege of ministers to play a central part in the planning and preparation of this service, a privilege which helps cement the minister's relationship to the families of the congregation.

As times change those who anticipate making their vows often look for new ways to express the old tradition. There have been countless innovations in the creation of marriage services, but those which seem to be most meaningful and most appropriate are the ones which effectively combine the traditional with a personal touch — the personality and character of the couple entering marriage.

While marriage homilies are seldom remembered by the jittery couple, they are often reviewed on video tapes during anniversary celebrations years after the event. It behooves the clergy to consider carefully the words they share on these occasions.

This collection of classics was first published many years ago. It is updated here with several additions and suggestions for including a personal flavor to the marriage service.

In addition to the numerous wedding homilies included here, there are two suggested orders of worship for the wedding service as well as a service for the celebration of a fiftieth wedding anniversary.

The authors of these meditations represent a variety of denominations.

A Personal Approach

By Thomas W. Lentz

After thirty years of working in parish ministry, I have gradually changed my approach to the wedding homily from "telling the couple how to live the best married life" to "celebrating what gifts they have discovered in each other."

As part of the pre-marriage counseling process I ask each one to fill out a form in which they answer or complete the following:

The thing that I first noticed about _____ (your future spouse) was _____

_____

_____

What made me fall in love with him/her was _____

_____

_____

The things I like about him/her are _____

_____

_____

I know that I want to spend the rest of my life with _____ because _____

_____

You may write anything else you wish about your personal feelings of love and affection for your future wife/husband.

From this material I compose the central part of the homily, concluding each part with the words "these are fine qualities that _____ has observed in you and they will serve you well as her husband (or as his wife)."

Obviously the material taken from these forms has to be chosen carefully. Some state facts that are too intimate for inclusion in a wedding homily. Others are simply inappropriate.

On the first year anniversary I mail the couple both of their statements and suggest that they enjoy a quiet meal together, reflecting upon the feelings they shared at the time of their wedding.

Because I ask each one to write the form confidentially, it is often a moment of surprise and joy in the wedding ceremony for each one to hear what the other has said.

Contemporary Wedding Service

By Leslie F. Brandt

(A contemporary wedding ceremony for the author's daughter)

Processional: "Joyful, Joyful, We Adore Thee"

Hymn: "Joyful, Joyful, We Adore Thee"

Responsive Reading: Contemporary Psalm 33

P: God is here — let's celebrate!

**C: With song and with dance,
With stringed instruments and brass,
With cymbals and drums.
Let us express our ecstatic joy in God's presence.**

P: Let us celebrate with old songs of praise.

**C: Let us also create new songs that portray the eternal love of
our God.**

P: He did create this world.

C: He continues to permeate it with his love.

P: Even amongst its distortions, its frustrated and unbelieving children,

C: He constantly carries out his purposes.

P: His plans for his world and its inhabitants

C: **Are not obliterated by the foolishness of men.**

P: His truth is not blotted out

C: **By the lethargy or lies of his apathetic creatures.**

P: He continues to reign over us.

C: **And to reveal himself to us.**

P: And God continues to create and to renew the world about us.

C: **He does this through those who relate to him,**
Who rely on his ever-present love.

P: He delivers his children from the fear of death and through them gives life to this world.

C: **God's love is sure and everlasting.**

P: The hearts that are open to his love are filled with joy.

C: **They truly find cause for celebration.**[1]

Exhortation:
Love has been a very popular and essential ingredient for life ever since Adam and Eve. Today we recognize more than ever before that what the world needs is love. In our day of computers and satellites, dehumanization and depersonalization has set in and is threatening to destroy us all. The single hope for our civilization is that we truly learn how to love.

What I refer to as love, however, is something much deeper and far more profound than what the world prescribes or many marriages demonstrate in our day. Paul aptly described its real content in his first Letter to the Church at Corinth when he wrote: "I may speak in tongues of men or of angels, but if I am without love, I am a sounding gong or a clanging cymbal. I may have the gift of prophecy, and know every hidden truth; I may have faith strong enough to move mountains; but if I have no love, I am nothing. I may dole out all I possess, or even give my body to be burnt, but if I have no love, I am none the better. Love is patient; love is kind and envies no one. Love is never boastful, nor conceited, nor rude; never selfish, nor quick to make offense. Love keeps no score of wrongs; does not gloat over other men's sins, but delights in the truth. There is nothing love cannot face; there is no limit to its faith, its hope, and its endurance. Love will never come to an end" (NEB).

Kahlil Gibran writes of some other facets of genuine love:

> *For even as love crowns you so shall he crucify you.*
> *Even as he is for your growth so is he for your pruning.*
> *Even as he ascends to your height and caresses your tenderest branches that quiver in the sun,*
> *So shall he descend to your roots and shake them in their clinging to the earth.*
> *Like sheaves of corn he gathers you unto himself.*
> *He threshes you to make you naked.*
> *He sifts you to free you from your husks.*
> *He grinds you to whiteness.*
> *He kneads you until you are pliant;*
> *And then he assigns you to his sacred fire, that you may become sacred bread for God's sacred feast ...*
> *But if in your fear you would seek only love's peace and love's pleasure,*
> *Then it is better for you that you cover your nakedness and pass out of love's threshing floor,*
> *Into the seasonless world where you shall laugh, but not all of your laughter, and weep, but not all of your tears.*
> *Love gives naught but itself and takes naught but from itself.*
> *Love possesses not nor would it be possessed;*
> *For love is sufficient unto love.*[2]

Because we are human and fallible creatures, this necessitates intense effort in the art of loving. It entails the will to love, the discipline needed daily to keep heart and mind set on loving. It requires great concentration. It demands much patience and understanding. Courage is a requirement for those who would be proficient in the art of loving. We may at times have to love in scorn of consequences. Faith is essential, faith in God's acceptances of us, in his promises to us, and in his power to use us in reaching others and thereby demonstrating his love for them. Tolerance is necessary in our acceptance of others. We must cease to be judgmental or condemnatory. We are not expected to condone wrongdoing. We must sometimes tolerate it in our acceptance of people as persons. We must love without the guarantee that those we love will respond or accept our love.

You, _____ and _____, are giving yourselves to each other in love. God forbid that you ever cease to specialize in and concentrate on the art of loving. And God forbid that your love be focused only upon each other — for then it becomes something less than love. May God grant that your love for each other be the consequence of your personal encounter with God — and that it may reach out to embrace others in sympathy and concern and touch them with the healing power of authentic love.

And now, in the name of the Father, the Son and the Holy Spirit, I ask you, _____, will you take _____ to be your wife and live with her in openness and love under God and his will for your lives?

_____, will you take _____ to be your husband and live with him in openness and love under God and his will for your lives?

Let us proceed to the altar where you may with promise and prayer commit yourselves to God and to each other in the blessed union of marriage.

Vows: *(Turn to each other and repeat in unison)*

I, _____, draw you unto my very being to share with you life's sorrows and joys. I promise to respect you and be respected by you, to forgive you and be forgiven by you, to instill hope in you and to be given hope by you. I promise to accept and to love you as you are in all that you are and, enriched and empowered by God's love, to seek and to follow, with you, his will and purpose for our lives.

Receiving of Rings
(Joining of right hands; pastor places his hand on theirs.)
    Now that _____ and _____ have consented to join together in the relationship of marriage, and have declared such before God and this assembly, I now pronounce them husband and wife, in the name of the Father, Son, and Holy Spirit.
    May our loving God, who created our first parents and sanctified their union in marriage, sanctify and bless you, that you may both please him in body and soul and live together in love until life's end. Amen.
    Let us now commune with God in Sacrament and in prayer.

(Couple kneels at altar. Soloist sings traditional "Let Us Break Bread Together." Pastor gives Words of Institution as he serves the bread and wine.)

Prayer
    Our great and loving God, whose eternal love has now united _____ and _____ in the relationship of marriage, who has heard their rededication to your will and purposes and touched and strengthened them with the bread and the wine, the body and the blood of Jesus Christ, grant them now and forever the grace to live in accordance with your word and to follow together in your footsteps. Sustain them in their faith and affection toward each other; watch over them and keep them amidst all the trials and temptations of this life. Send them forth as your servants to exemplify and demonstrate toward each other and in their relationships to their fellowmen your great love for all humanity about them. We commit them to your care, O God, through Jesus Christ, your Son, our Lord, who lives and reigns with you and the Holy Spirit, one God, within our world today. Amen.

Soloist: Prayer anthem (or Lord's Prayer)

13

Benediction

Recessional: "Lord Of The Dance"

---

1. Contemporary Psalm 33: Leslie F. Brandt, *God Is Here — Let's Celebrate!*

2. Kahlil Gibran, *The Prophet* (New York: Alfred A. Knopf, 1969), pp. 12, 13, 14.

Marital Horticulture

By John M. Braaten

_____ and _____ we have gathered together this afternoon just for you. We have come, at your invitation, to hear you express your love for each other and to witness the making of your sacred vows. We are thrilled for you on this beautiful day as you step into the future as husband and wife.

We are mindful that fantasy is usually involved in thinking about a wedding. However, marriage is not a whimsical experience. So I ask you, and forgive me if it sounds brutal, "So what?" So what if your wedding today is a beautiful affair if, in a year or in ten years, your marriage withers and dies? So what if you are today caught up in ecstasy, if at some future day you find yourself regretting this very hour? The questions may seem unkind, but they are realistic. Almost one out of every two marriages ends in divorce. As one cynic put it, "If marriages are made in heaven, God's doing a pretty lousy job these days."

Of course you and I know that marriages aren't made in heaven. They're made on earth by young and sinful human beings. And unless the persons who make up a relationship are willing to sacrifice, to work _for_ each other, and to forgive one another, their marriage will certainly fail. Romance cannot hold a marriage together. Only unselfish love can do that.

Let me illustrate by means of a homely parable. A couple goes out to plant a seed: a seed which, they hope, will grow into a beautiful and healthy plant. The seed is lovingly cared for as it is sown. It is watered and watched over anxiously. Then one day the seed germinates. It breaks the ground, thrusting its leaves upward. What a day of celebration! The flower is growing. Then, seeing that the plant is established, the couple leaves it to itself and no longer attends its needs. Soon weeds close in, garden pests attack, and diseases infect it. Because the plant lacks sufficient water and nutrients, it slowly but surely shrivels and dies.

You have probably guessed by now that the parable is really the story of a love relationship. When two people become serious about each other, the seed of love is planted. During courtship they foster that love. They feel anxiety over their relationship and strive to make it grow by pleasing the other. Then comes the wedding day. The seedling of their love breaks the ground and their love becomes public in a wedding ceremony. But the *plant* of their marriage must be cared for if it is to survive. Unless the weeds of selfishness, pride, and mistrust are rooted out, the marriage will have to struggle to grow. Unless the diseases of pettiness and stubbornness are arrested, the marriage will never become as beautiful as God designed it to be. Unless the marriage is exposed to the sunlight of love and affection, it will become stunted and weak. Unless it is generously nourished with words of forgiveness and encouragement, it will surely die.

You see, _____ and _____, the seedling of your love has just broken the surface on this day. Today is not the culmination of your romance; it is but the beginning. All you have done, all you have meant to each other; has been preparation. The growth of your marriage, and its blossoming into beauty, will depend upon what you do from this day forward.

As your family and friends, we have great hopes and dreams for your marriage, just as you do. But we know that wedded bliss doesn't just happen. You will have to work hard in the garden of your marriage if it is to grow and flourish. That is why I suggest you take the psalmist's words to heart: "Blessed are those who fear the Lord, who walk in his ways! You shall eat the fruit of the labor of your hands; you shall be happy, and it shall be well with you" (Psalm 128:1-2).

These words are not intended as crop insurance as much as they are words of gardening advice from an agricultural expert. He knows what he's talking about. He advises you to stay close to God. For God's presence in a marriage is like water to a plant. He comes to shower receptive hearts with unique and rich blessings. In experiencing his forgiveness and love we are motivated to be forgiving and loving toward one another. We know that plants grow best in warm weather. Only God can add the warmth that will make the *plant* of your marriage grow lush and beautiful, its fragrance embellishing the lives of all who are touched by it.

Make no mistake. The cultivation of your marriage is still up to you. Even if marriages were made in heaven, they would still need to be lived out on earth. In marriage, God gives you the responsibility for the care and keeping of the other. You are to love, forgive, share, and communicate his great love. In a sense, God's love takes on human form through your relationship as husband and wife. It is an awesome responsibility, but it can be a great joy, and it can make of your marriage a flower of wondrous beauty, one which is able to decorate the world for the glory of God.

So we urge you never to forget your responsibilities toward each other on behalf of your Creator and Redeemer. And I commend these words to you as you leave this place to begin work in the garden of your marriage: you will be blessed, _____ and _____, if you live respectfully before the Lord and walk in his ways. You will eat the fruit of the labor of your hands. You will be happy, and it will be well with you.

To that end, God bless you today and forever. Amen.

Married To The Holy One Of Israel

By William J. Rauch

An old and experienced rabbi snuggled back into an overstuffed airplane seat, quite prepared to sleep during the flight to a far away city. But the young man beside him seemed anxious for a dialogue. This man has never talked to a Jewish person before, much less to a rabbi. After some preliminary conversation, the young man asked: "Sir , what is the message of your religion?" Without a moment's hesitation the rabbi replied: "God is Israel's husband." And with that the Rabbi fell off to sleep. He had said it all.

The Bible doesn't say much about marriage. The Scriptures *do not* provide the ritual for the wedding service. In fact, the Bible doesn't even have a requirement that a minister must be present at a wedding. The Old Testament does contain a few regulations dealing with marriage and family problems. And in the New Testament Jesus talks about marriage on several occasions, particularly in terms of the question of divorce. But that's about it! The Bible talks about married people and recognizes the need for the institution of marriage, but the Bible does not define the meaning of marriage except in a few, important passages.

The aged rabbi was right! The Old Testament does picture God as married to Israel:

> *... for your husband is your maker, whose name is the LORD of Hosts; your ransomer is the holy One of Israel, who is called God of all earth.*   Isaiah 54:5 (NEB)

Marriage is the most intimate relationship of human life. The Old Testament is well aware of its intimacy. One of the Bible words for the sexual relationship is the word, "know."

> *Now Adam knew Eve his wife and she conceived and bore ... .*   Genesis 4:1 (RSV)

The partners in a marriage relationship "knew" all about each other. They become aware of every quirk and habit of each other. They learn the thinking patterns of the other person so well that they can begin to predict the behavior of their mate. It's for that reason that the Old Testament pictures God as the husband of his people. He knows us better than we know ourselves. He is the most intimate participant in all of the events of our lives.

The New Testament spells out this relationship even more clearly:

> *Husbands, love your wives, as Christ also loved the church and gave himself up for it, to consecrate it ... In the same way men also are bound to love their wives as they love their own bodies. In loving his wife a man loves himself. For no one ever hated his own body: on the contrary he provides and cares for it; and that is how Christ treats the church, because it is his body, of which we are living parts. Thus it is that (in the words of Scripture) "a man shall leave his father and mother and shall be joined to his wife, and the two shall become one flesh." It is a great truth that is hidden here. I for my part refer it to Christ and to the church, but it applies also individually: each of you must love his wife as his very self; and the woman must see to it that she pays her husband all respect.*
> Ephesians 5:25, 28-33 (NEB)

Saint Paul seems to be using marriage as a sermon to get his point across about Christ. But notice that he also says: "But it applies also individually: each of you must love his wife as his very self; and the woman must see to it that she pays her husband all respect." In other words, the union of husband and wife in marriage somehow becomes a mysterious experience of the union of Christ and his people. From their marriage, a husband and wife learn of their relationship with Christ. Christ's church is built up by reciprocal sharing and sacrificial love. Good marriages have both sharing and love, just as does the church. The church is a living example to the husband and wife of the potential of their marriage. Commitment to Christ brings about love in marriage, and the alliance of husband and wife teach us of how we should respond to Christ.

And so today we celebrate two kinds of marriage at the same time. We witness the fact _____ and _____ are to be husband and wife for a lifetime. We also celebrate the truth that we are all married to God through Christ for all eternity.

From Guest To Member

By Gary C. Bratz

Text: Luke 19:5-6: *When Jesus came to the place he looked up and said to him, "Zacchaeus, hurry and come down; for I must stay at your house today." So he hurried down and was happy to welcome him.* (NRSV)

_____ and _____, I know this is a happy day for both of you. And it ought to be, because in the divinely ordained estate of marriage, your love for each other finds its greatest fulfillment, as you become one flesh and one spirit.

When God created man, he said, "It is not good for man to be alone. I will make a help-meet for him." The word "help-meet" means one who is fit for him, one who will make him a whole person. And so God made a wife for Adam, someone to complement him. One person alone is never a whole person, never a compete person. As you take each other as husband and wife, you will become one unit, one flesh, one complete person. So strong and so wonderful is the tie that binds you together in marriage.

It's a happy day for you, too, because you are united not only with each other, but also with Jesus Christ, your Lord. It is he who courted you, who pleaded with you to accept him, and who claimed you as his own. It is he upon whom life is founded and upon whom your marriage should be built.

A marriage is only as strong as are the marriage partners. You, as Christians, know this — and that's why you want Christ, your Lord. It is he who courted you, who pleaded with you to accept him, and who claimed you as his own. It is he upon whom life is founded and upon whom your marriage should be built.

A marriage is only as strong as are the marriage partners. You, as Christians, know this — and that's why you want Christ with you in your marriage. For he it is that will give you strength when you are weak; who will make you loving when you feel more like quarreling; who will make you charitable when you want to hurt.

Our text doesn't speak about marriage, or about anyone who is about to be married. But it says something to married people. Zacchaeus wanted to see Jesus, and because the crowd around Jesus was so thick he had to climb a tree. When Jesus passed by him, he said to Zacchaeus, "Hurry and come down; I must come and stay with you."

This is what Jesus is saying to you today. Just as with Zacchaeus, Jesus wants to enter your home, too, and stay with you — not just as an occasional guest, but as a lifetime resident. He, who redeemed you with his own blood, wants to enter your home and provide you with the strength you need to live together in harmony and peace and real love.

Zacchaeus climbed down quickly and welcomed Jesus gladly. May you do the same. As you desire to make your home a Christ-centered and Christ-lived-in home, you will acknowledge your allegiance to Christ in your worship life, as Sunday after Sunday finds you worshiping together in God's house, and day after day finds you reading God's Word together and praying together.

As a Christ-centered home you will also be a serving family, encouraging by your example the principle of helping others and sharing family joys and privileges with those less fortunate.

Your home, with Christ living in it, will set an example. It will be a working unit that demonstrates what life together can be like in a Christian world.

May you, too, then welcome Christ gladly into your home. Accept him and his promises, seek him for his help, and trust in him as your Savior.

_____ and _____, my prayer shall be, on this your wedding day, that Christ will always live with thee, today, tomorrow, every day.

As now you enter wedded life, and into this glorious state now come, may both of you, as man and wife, welcome Christ into your home. As did Zacchaeus, so may you, gladly welcome Christ to stay, not just as a guest, but a member, too, forevermore, from this glad day. Amen.

Marriage Likened To A Wedding Cake

By Richard E. Boye

_____ and _____, it might be said that a Christian marriage is like the beautiful and tasty wedding cake you will soon enjoy. Part of the reason for this is that both Christian marriage and the wedding cake must have the right ingredients if they are to be the delight to body and soul they are meant to be.

One essential ingredient for a joyous matrimonial union is **humility**. Many of life's doors are closed to the proud, but the very same doors are opened by the grace of humility. Let me mention just one thing in particular. Once there stood a humble man in the Temple not far from a proud man, and this humble man prayed, "God, be merciful to me a sinner." In effect, he was speaking to God two words that stick in the throats of every proud man. He was saying, "I'm sorry." Because he was able to say that sincerely, his relationship with God was deepened. That kind of humility is no elective if marriage is to be all that it can be. As you move now from the springtime of your lives toward autumn, if you want your union together to be a joy instead of a burden, you must be prepared repeatedly to swallow your pride so that the words, "I'm sorry" can pass through your lips. Thus, your relationship together will not be fractured by pride. Instead, you will be welded ever closer together in a deep and meaningful relationship.

Another ingredient you dare not do without is **growth**. Many of the people I counsel have ceased to grow, but that is not the worst of it. Actually, such people are missing out on much fun in life. I know people in their sixties who are actually intellectual and emotional children, and just because of this life's deepest joys are passing them by. In particular, their marriages have become dull instead of that which God intended — namely, an ever more exciting relationship as each year passes by. A familiar verse, the end of which everybody knows, begins thus: "And Jesus increased...." That is, the Master himself grew, and the rest of the verse tells

how: "in wisdom and in stature, and in favor with God and man."
What a splendid outline for life at its best! Since we cannot stand
still even if we try, I urge you to increase, that is, to continue growing into a bigger person. Grow in *maturity*, or you will regress into
childish ways. Grow in *communication* with each other, or you
will become less able to talk together. Grow in *usefulness* to the
world and to one another, or selfishness will get the better of you.
Grow in *knowledge,* or you will be left behind in ignorance. Grow
in *interestingness*, or you will become a bore to be with and a cause
for your mate to find his or her satisfactions elsewhere. In short, let
the leaven of growth raise you to your full potential as a person
and consequently as a marital partner also.

Still another ingredient for a happy home, as you might expect,
is **love**. This is as important to a marriage as flour is to a cake.
Right now, quite naturally, there is an aura of romantic love sur-
rounding the two of you. We rejoice in this. Yet, it will take more
than romantic love to carry you all the way through to your golden
years. The two of you and all of us, too, need a love from on high,
lest our homes be somehow blighted. Such love is "patient and
kind." It is "not jealous or boastful; it is not arrogant or rude." This
"love does not insist on its own way; it is not irritable or resentful;
it does not rejoice at wrong, but rejoices in the right." This love,
which Paul holds so beautifully before us, "bears all things, be-
lieves all things, hopes all things, endures all things." What is more,
we are promised that this "love never ends." Now, of course, it is
easy to see that this profound and enduring kind of love is just
what any marriage needs to rise up to its joyous best.

But one things needs yet to be said. The right ingredients, humility, growth, and love, fine as they be, are still not enough. Even
as a wedding cake needs a master baker to blend and to bake, so
marriage, even though it may have the right ingredients, needs God
to put them there and to increase with his Spirit. God *can* and *will*
make your marriage both beautiful to behold and a delight to your
persons if you will but be receptive. Think about that. Pray about
it. *Only* in this way will your marriage be a mounting joy "so long
as ye both shall live."

Marriage Is Joy

By Kenneth H. Sauer

(Homily for a seminarian who was being married in a service with Eucharist)

Weddings are times of great joy. Even our tears are tears of joy. Perhaps no other occasions produce such gladness.

And yet if we seek the reason — we are bewildered. We don't really know exactly why marriage is such a wonderfully joyful time, but we know!

The Bible gives us a hint at the reason. Both Jesus and Paul quote the verse in Genesis which says, "Did you know that he which made them at the beginning made them male and female and said ... for this reason a man leaves father and mother...."

The reason marriage is such a joyful time is that it announces the fulfillment of life for a man and a woman.

God has made us male and female in such a way that we do not discover our truest humanness without the other.

Adam is not the word for one man, but ***humanity***. Man plus Woman, in the understanding of the Bible, equals humanity. We join humanity, begin to experience the totality of what God aims for his children in the life together in marriage.

So we rejoice for _____ and _____ this day that they embark on life together in marriage.

But when we ask what the constant of life together in marriage is all about we often find ourselves in a quandary. Around us many say, marriage is quarreling, resentment, infidelity, inhibition, unhappiness. Around us many say I can find the truest fulfillment of my life without the encumbrances of marriage, without the responsibilities of a husband or wife.

What makes us so certain that marriage is joy?

Paul had an idea! The dynamic of marriage is similar, he says, to the relationship of members of the Church and Christ. Christians

25

know that Christ loves them, that Christ has blessed them with many gifts, that Christ has even died for them. They know that Christ wants the best for them as they live in the Church. They know that Christ wants to help them reflect God's love in their lives. Therefore Christians trust Christ, they are willing to go wherever Christ leads them, they submit all their own desires and goals to that of Christ and his people.

And the wonder of it is that in just this kind of self-giving, the Christian finds joy and fulfillment and a sense of accomplishment and freedom.

Now, says Paul, this same experience happens in marriage. The wife also knows that her husband loves her, wants to care for her, and wants to help her find the best in life. For this reason she can give herself to him in trust and service.

Now Paul is saying nothing about a woman's legal or social status, her physical capacity or achievements, or her education or emancipation. He is saying that all these things will never change the fact that she is, and remains, woman. She has a place and vocation to fulfill that goes with her creation by God, and this is what Paul is talking about.

The husband also has a unique vocation, just as Christ did. In marriage the husband's vocation is to lead, provide, strengthen, and protect, with the aim of helping his beloved become her best self.

Because marriage unites husband and wife in a one-flesh relationship, the wife becomes part of the husband and his care for her is the same as the care he would have for his own person, because in fact she has become joined to him.

As Christ nourishes his body, the Church, through his Word and Sacraments, through his presence with his people, so the husband nourishes his wife and family through his work and gifts and love, and presence with them.

Mutual subjection in love is the dynamic of Christian living, and it finds its clearest illustration in the life of marriage.

Yet we know full well that we are all sinners and our failings are ever before us. That is why we have this marriage held in the Church, and why we ask God's blessings and receive his gifts of forgiveness and love in the Holy Communion. We need this abundant blessing to fulfill our vocation as husband and wife.

Paul may not really help us much because he uses one mystery to illustrate another. Of marriage, Paul says, I understand it applies to Christ and the Church. But he says, **it also applies to you.**

Only in this mysterious relationship of life-together-in-marriage, and life-together with Christ in his Church, can we begin to understand what both are all about. Someone has said, "You don't learn about marriage from books; you learn by being married." And you don't learn about God's love by reading about it, but receiving it.

So, the joy and the dynamic of the life _____ and _____ begin today is a discovery that they will make in their life together in love, and then service to the Lord in his Church.

The Dean of Seminary and his wife celebrated their fiftieth anniversary of marriage while I was there, and it was revealed that on the inside of their wedding rings they had both inscribed these words: Each for the other, and both for God.

That is what Paul was trying to say — that is what we say today, that is our reason for rejoicing for _____ and _____ this day. Amen.

One Husband's Counsel

By John M. Braaten

_____ and _____, what a marvelous day this is for us! In this moment we have come to stand by you as, in the presence of our Lord, you experience one of the most precious and important events of your life — your wedding. We are here to assure you that because we love you, we will pray for you and support you as you go out from this place. For we know that happy weddings are a dime a dozen; happy marriages are rare.

Unfortunately, there are no self-help books, no "Ten Steps to Marital Bliss" which can ensure a strong, joyous marriage. But Saint Peter in his first letter gives some sound words of wisdom. Peter, you might recall, is the only disciple who we know for sure was married. Listen to his husbandly counsel. "... Have unity of spirit, sympathy, love of [each other], a tender heart and a humble mind. Do not return evil for evil or [insult for insult]; but on the contrary bless, for to this you have been called, that you may obtain a blessing" (1 Peter 3:8-9).

Peter, as a husband, knows that a good marriage takes more than determination; it requires selfless love, patience, and self-sacrifice. It also takes an awareness that a married couple is, in fact, a single entity. So he speaks of having unity of spirit.

It's a fact. Your lives are now so inextricably bound that every action and every word, directly or indirectly affects the other. You have great power over each other, power to make the other either happy or depressed. But you cannot cause sorrow to your mate without losing something of the dignity and beauty of love in the process, just as you cannot bring happiness without adding to your own enjoyment of life. As you become united in marriage, you hold the emotions of each other in your hands. God grant you the wisdom to hold them gently, with compassion.

Peter also counsels you to have sympathy, and stresses how important this is in a good marriage. To know that someone stands by you, no matter how rugged and rough the times become, is a great blessing. One thing is clear: sympathy and selfishness cannot occupy the same space. Sympathy requires that we forget ourselves, step outside ourselves, and identify with the cares and problems of our mate. It is within the arena of sympathy and compassion that love grows deeper and more lovely than any newlyweds can possibly imagine.

Another point of Peter's counsel is to remain humble. Sad is the marriage when one or both of the spouses think they could have done better or feel they got the raw end of the marriage. It can happen. It is very easy to take our mate for granted, to forget virtues, and to concentrate on faults. We are all sinful and imperfect people, who are difficult to live with at times. Never lose the capacity to marvel at the fact that your mate chose to marry you, warts and all!

Then Peter counsels you to be forgiving. Forgiveness is the heart of happiness. We know that hostility upsets our bodies and our lives. To be at odds with one's mate creates an agony which consumes our energy and dominates our thoughts. Strange, then, that we do not seek reconciliation more readily. I assure you, you will save much time and emotional wear and tear by being willing to seek reconciliation. Do not return evil for evil or insult for insult; be mature enough to reach out to each other with forgiveness and love.

Paul concludes his counsel by urging you to be a blessing. The best way this happens is to create a home in which Christ is present. Attending worship together has a cohesive influence on a relationship; devotions together brings some of the most healing interludes of life. Opening our hearts and our home to Christ in no way diminishes our happiness in marriage — far from it — for he brings his blessing and joy and peace wherever he resides. And you know, the more you revel in his blessings, the more of a blessing you will be to each other and to all whose lives are graced by yours.

So then, _____ and _____, we are sending you off with our prayers and our love. In following the counsel of Peter, may you discover all the great and wonderful things that

God has planned for your future. As you do, you will truly be a blessing to each other, to your loved ones, and to your God. May he watch over your days and your deeds in his peace. Amen.

Accept Our Failures

By Leslie F. Brandt

Something that we must learn as we progress through life is the importance of being imperfect. Most of us are very frightened by failure. The struggle of life is generally the struggle for success. We tend to forget that our Lord came to redeem failures, not successes, and only failures are eligible for his good gifts of grace.

When there is no other way out, most of us will reluctantly admit to imperfections. We then quickly latch on to someone's observation that we humans are a strange and unique mixture of shame and splendor. We ought to recognize right from the start that successful marital relations are very much dependent upon our ability to accept our mates as they are, with their imperfections, and that real trouble sets in when we insist on moulding them into some pattern, probably distorted by our own imperfections, that we concoct. No matter whom we marry, should we have the world of men or women from which to choose, our mates just will not turn out to be as strong and affectionate or masculine or tender or thoughtful or intelligent or honest or capable or motivated as we had imagined or wished. Of course, they do offer some pleasant surprises in regards to some traits, but there are others where they will fall short of expectations which may in themselves be distorted. It is when we lovingly accept our mate's shortcomings as well as assets that marriage takes on a secure basis, and we can learn how to love one another. Then the so-called honeymoon is over, and we can get down to the business of enjoying as well as enduring each other as married mates.

Before we can accept, and perhaps even learn to respect, the imperfections of others, at least to give others the right to be imperfect, we must learn how to accept our own. This does not mean that we cherish them or even condone them, but that we seek to recognize them and be aware of them. Some of them are cause for sorrow and shame, but even they do not subtract from our value

31

and significance as persons. In reality, it is the failure or inability to recognize, admit, and face up with them that gives these distortions the power to cripple us and render us ineffective as humans or mates. In the psychological frame of reference, we learn how to utilize our strong points of character to compensate for or to overcome our weak points. In the Christian framework, we are challenged to recognize and to allow our weaknesses to drive us to the supernatural resources of God, who promises to transform them into vehicles of his divine power and grace. In other words, our imperfections do not have to be our undoing. They can be useful in directing our lives toward effectiveness and happiness. This can be done only if we have the wisdom and the courage to face them, accept them as a part of our sin-permeated nature, deal with them with our endowed intelligence, and the grace made available to us in Jesus Christ, and realize that they do not make us less worthy or significant as God's children.

As human beings, we have the right to fail, and the right to be imperfect. But as we have the right to fail, so do our mates. We are all a part of this sinful human race. Once we understand and accept ourselves as failures in need of divine grace, we should have little trouble in identifying with our mates along with their distortions and imperfections.

The thing that makes all this possible is the grace of God that specializes in turning liabilities into assets and that can transform the shame of human failure into the splendor of Christian effectiveness. It is to this God as manifested in Jesus Christ that I commend you. If you individually and mutually make him your focal point and adopt his purposes as your purposes, your relationship will be genuine and secure.

A Prayer For Your Marriage

By Robert Howard Clausen

(This wedding address was for a young couple, both active members of the church.)

Text: Ephesians 3:14-19

Dear Christian Friends,

In the lesson before us we have a beautiful and moving prayer by the apostle Paul for the people of the church of Ephesus whom he knew well and loved much.

By extension, under the inspiration of God's Holy Spirit, the words of Holy Scripture set down by Paul become a prayer for all of God's people in all ages of the Church's history.

It is meant for each one of us here present who bow our knees unto the God and Father of our Lord Jesus Christ, of whom the whole family — and this means the fellowship of believers — is named.

On this occasion, in this setting, we can apply it most directly, _____ and _____, to your situation, as you stand before God's altar to speak your wedding vows.

It becomes, very personally, a prayer for your marriage. There are four parts to this prayer.

First, "That he would grant you, according to the riches of his glory, to be strengthened with might by his Spirit in the inner man" (v. 16).

This is an act of God's grace. God, by his Spirit, has given you new birth in your baptism; he has put faith in your hearts; and he has led you to know and to receive his Son as your Savior. He has made you heirs of heaven. God has continued faithful, and has kept you in the true faith.

Now, as you are joined by him in marriage, God the Holy Spirit will continue to provide you with the resources of God's grace, helping you to remain faithful to your promises to God and to one another, helping you to find and to do God's will in your married life together.

As Christians, we are realistic. We know that evil is abroad in the world. We know that the infection of sin in this fallen creation is all-pervasive. We know the weakness of our old nature.

As you face the future together you know there will be pressures from the world, tensions within you, and frictions between you. There will be problems, pains, and disappointments. There will sometimes be agonizing adjustments to new loyalties and new responsibilities. The inner man, the inner woman, renewed in Christ will know weariness, weakness, edginess, fretfulness.

Take heart. The Holy Spirit is at hand to strengthen you, to revive you, to refresh you, to invest you with new vigor spiritually, physically, and emotionally so that you may continue to work with energy and dedication toward the true fulfillment of your married life.

Second, this prayer asks "that Christ may dwell in your hearts by faith" (v. 17).

The continuing, abiding presence of Christ in your hearts will make the difference between a marriage of form and a marriage of true spiritual meaning. This indwelling of Christ is surely a mark of God's grace. It is the assurance of sins forgiven, a testimony of God's abiding good will toward you.

But the indwelling Christ is also evidence that your hearts are changed in outlook and attitude. The apostle Paul says elsewhere that we are to have "the mind of Christ." This means Christ's attitude. His obedience to the will of God the Father, his concern for the Father's work, his compassion for people, his sensitivity to other's needs are to be the pattern of our thinking and doing. He himself said, "He that abideth in me, and I in him, the same bringeth forth much fruit; for without me ye can do nothing" (John 15:5).

The indwelling of Christ in our hearts by faith is assured when we open our hearts to the means of grace which God has given us.

Together, you will share the Word of God. Together, you will kneel to receive the Sacrament of Christ's Body and Blood. Through these channels God will act to make the presence of Christ in your hearts by faith more forceful and real.

Third, the prayer continues, "that ye being rooted and grounded in love, may be able to comprehend, with all saints, what is the breadth and length and depth and heights, and to know the love of Christ, which passeth knowledge" (vv. 17-19).

You are rooted and grounded in your love for one another, and this is valuable and good. God will bless, honor and sanctify that love as you consecrate it to him day by day.

But to find your most complete unity and ablest support for the burdens, responsibilities, and joys of marriage, we need to be rooted and grounded in a greater love — God's love for us.

May we never fail to see the measure of that love as it has been expressed in Jesus Christ. "To know" this love means to experience it in a personal way. "God commandeth his love for us in that while we were yet sinners, Christ died for us" (Romans 5:8)

God's love, as we see it in Christ, is a complete giving of oneself for the sake of the beloved. The more that we know, understand and experience the love of Christ, the more we will know the kind of love we must give to one another — not selfish, demanding, critical, and repressive, but free, helpful, open, and seeking the fulfillment of one another's personality as a son, a daughter of God in Jesus Christ.

Our love will serve.

Our love will absorb hurt.

Our love will forgive.

Our love will share.

Our love will comfort.

Our love will support.

And our love, as we seek it, will be replenished from the resources of God's boundless love.

Fourth, the prayer concludes, "that ye might be filled with the fulness of God."

This is God's plan for us. To be filled with "the fulness of God" is to become true people.

The Enemy, Satan, would drain us of life and set us on the way of death, perverting our energies and warping our personalities.

Christ exhibits true humanity in all its beauty and Godlike wonder. We are to grow in to him, by God's grace, maturing each day as God's people, being filled with the fulness of God. We want this for each other. We want to help each other to this end.

Therefore, as husband and wife, encourage one another in the faith. Pray for and with one another. Set a Christ-like example for one another. See Christ in each other.

And carry this prayer for your marriage from your wedding day into all your days together, trusting that God will hear, answer, strengthen, and bless you through his Son, Jesus Christ, our Lord. Amen.

The Mathematics of Marriage

By William McKee Aber

(Written for the wedding of two college students. Modern music and Communion were a part of the service, but the meditation could be used in any wedding service where a homily is requested.)

Order Of Service For The Wedding

Processional

Call To Worship And Betrothal followed the traditional opening sections of the United Presbyterian marriage service, concluding with the couple promising to "have each other in the holy bond of marriage."

Hymn "Let us Break Bread Together On Our Knees"

Prayer Of Confession

Assurance of Pardon in traditional words by the pastor

Sacrament of Holy Communion shared by wedding party and congregation, while music was played.

The Meditation*

The Marriage Vows and Exchange Of Rings using the traditional form of United Presbyterian Church.

Hymn "They'll Know We Are Christians By Our Love"

Pronouncement Of Marriage by the pastor.

Recessional

*The Mathematics Of Marriage

As Christians we find the basis for our faith in a unique kind of mathematics. We say that one equals three, and three equals one. By which we mean that we believe in one God, who shows himself to us in three diffrent persons — as Father, and as Son, and as Holy Spirit.

As we participate in Christian marriage, we discover once again a kind of unique mathematics — this time involving the addition of one and one. Surprisingly enough, as two persons come together, they become *one*. But they also are *two*. And, hopefully, they also are *three*. Let's look at the math.

One plus one equals one. This is the normal equation of marriage. Two persons come together, and they become one being. As long ago as the time of the writing of the Book of Genesis, this was a known fact. For we read there that "a man leaves his father and mother and cleaves to his wife, and they become one flesh." Two persons come together, and they become one. They become a new entity — a new being. They think new thoughts and do new things, for they are now together, and their love and concern for each other moves them in other directions than they moved in the past. Their actions are conditioned by, and often dependent upon, the feelings of each other.

Becoming one flesh means, of course, sharing the deepest sexual bonds. But it means much more than that. It means orienting your life so that your whole being is tied to your partner. It means being so open to another person that you are known fully by that person, accepted by that person, and loved by that person. And your identity is found in your involvement with that person. The two of you have become one.

And yet, as soon as we say that, we must also say that in marriage **one plus one still equals two**. We become one flesh in marriage; we find new meaning and life in the relationship that has been established — but we are still individuals. We still have our own thoughts, dreams, and hopes. Most of them we share, but Kahlil Gibran has put it wisely, I think, when he says, "Let there be spaces in your togetherness." He goes on to say,

Love one another, but make not a bond of love ...
Sing and dance together and be joyous, but let each one
    of you be alone ...
And stand together, yet not too near together:
For the pillars of the temple stand apart,
And the oak tree and the cypress grow not in each other's
    shadow[1]

It is important, even within marriage, that we remain individuals. For each one of us is a unique being and the essence of marriage is accepting the other, rather than overwhelming the other one! Even as God loves and accepts us as we are, so marriage is a place where we love and accept another being as he is. There needs to be "space in the togetherness" of marriage. There needs to be a time for privacy — a time for being oneself. And, strangely enough, by being oneself one becomes more able to be a part of the other person. He has more of himself to give.

But, the most important sum in a marriage is the fact that **one plus one equals three.** This could, of course, refer to the children that hopefully become a part of each marriage, but I'm thinking of something else today. I'm thinking of the fact that in our marriage there is a third party — namely, God. The essence of Christian marriage is that two separate individuals, while retaining their own identity, also receive a new identity in the oneness of marriage. But this is possible only when a third party is a vital part of that marriage; it is possible only when God's love and forgiveness becomes a reality within us.

The promise of the Christian faith is that God is indeed with us, in the person of Jesus Christ. So marriage finds meaning when Christ's presence is real. In him we discover forgiveness and acceptance; in him we discover understanding and forbearance; in him we are able to love. In fact, our ability to love comes from him: "We love, because he first loved us."

So marriage has its own mathematics. Two become one. Two remain two. Two become three. And the mathematics becomes real through the power of God.

---

1. Kahlil Gibran, *The Prophet* (New York: Alfred A. Knopf, 1946), pp. 16, 17.

Leeches Or Lovers

By Leslie F. Brandt

We can make grandiose statements about our willingness to forgive or to tolerate the atrocities of our fellowman, and may even demonstrate it among less intimate relationships about us, but when it comes to our most personal relationships — with those we love the most — our willingness or ability to forgive is often in question.

The most obvious explanation is that our professed love for our intimates is generally an adulterated love. In spite of the affection shown or the gifts given, the professions and the proclamations, our love is often self-centered rather than sacrificial. We love in response to love. Instead of loving others as ourselves, we love ourselves in others. We seek, unconsciously or otherwise, to possess those whom we profess to love. We draw our ego-strength from them. We are sometimes more like leeches than we are lovers. When those who are dear to us reach out to take from or give to others, it frightens us. We react in jealousy with hurt feelings and hostility. Instead of contributing to the independence and personhood of others, we unwittingly seek to rob them of what they have and tend to treat those close to us as things rather than persons — all in the name of love. We will live, even die for them, support and protect them, as long as they live within our structures and walk according to our strategies and respond to our childish needs.

All this is reflected in most human love-relationships, but the kind of love manifested and projected by Jesus Christ is very different and represents the kind of interpersonal relationships, and husband-wife relationships, that lead to personality, health, and happiness.

We must learn how to forgive those whom we love the most, but we can do so only if our love for them is an authentic love. This does not mean that we must condone our spouses' weaknesses. It

40

does mean that we love them irrespective of the flaws and failures in their lives, and that we allow them the right to make mistakes, to fail, and continue to be lovingly open and receptive to them. This kind of love or ability to love is not the natural possession of any person, but it is available to all. It comes by way of the forgiving and saving love of God as revealed in Jesus Christ. When we are absorbed in and by God's redeeming and regenerating love, we should be enabled to reflect such love in our interpersonal relationships. Thus it is to his love and grace that I commend you in this great moment of your lives.

Something Old, Something New, Something Borrowed, Something Blue

By Kenneth H. Sauer

(A general wedding homily built around the traditions)

There is nothing that happens in our society that is as filled with sentiment and custom as a marriage.

However, if a wedding is to have permanent significance in the lives of these young people, and for us, we need to see it in a deeper context than sentiment and custom.

We need to see marriage as **something old**. We didn't think it up — it's not new to our generation. It's old — as old as the origin of humankind.

> *He which made them at the beginning, made them male and female and said — for this cause shall a man leave his father and mother and cleave to his wife.*

God made us male and female — for the reason that there would be marriage. We are created for marriage — for life together. What happens here today is something old — these young people, _____ and _____ are fulfilling their created purpose in becoming man and wife.

In spite of the jokes — the attacks — the sin — which can beset marriage in our time, *we* can confidently rejoice in *this* marriage because it is rooted in the nature of things — it is the way God wills for his children.

We need to see marriage as **something new**!

> *A man leaves father and mother; a wife has her own home to care for.*

Marriage As Crisis

By Leslie F. Brandt

The time of marriage is a time of crisis. We usually associate the word "crisis" with something unfortunate. This is not necessarily true. It refers to something very important in one's life — and in this case — something very good. It is a crisis in that it is perhaps the most important decision and transaction you will ever make.

Two people, from different environments, with different personalities and natures, are deciding to walk intimately together through the rest of their lives. Together they are to face its conflicts as well as its moments of peace, its sufferings and sorrows as well as its joys, its failures as well as its successes. Statistics prove that it is a hazardous journey with pitfalls along the road, and a large percentage of such relationships are terminated by such pitfalls even before they are well launched.

The blessing of God upon your relationship at this, the first step of your marriage, is a good beginning, but it is by no means a guarantee that your relationship will be a successful one. There is only one guarantee: it is that you walk with God, dedicating yourselves individually and mutually to him and his will for your lives. The point is, you can't go this alone and hope to find perpetual happiness. You need God's help — and perhaps the help of qualified advisors that he may place in your path.

As you commit yourselves to each other — for better or for worse — commit yourselves totally and wholly to God and his purposes. You will find him sufficient for this glorious crisis of marriage, and for all the unhappy crises that may come your way.

45

We Belong To Each Other

By Kenneth H. Sauer

This is a great day for John and Susan, for their families, for friends. Even our tears are tears of joy and gladness for them and their future together.

The Bible tells us that our God rejoices for them, too. The Bible you know isn't only concerned with spiritual things. The Bible is concerned with the lives of people in the world with their joys — and yes, the love of a man for a woman. Why else would the Bible contain some of the loveliest love poems ever written, the Song of Songs?

In the eighth chapter of the Song of Songs there are these words:

> *Set me as a seal upon your heart,*
> *as a seal upon your arm:*
> *for love is strong as death,*
> *jealousy as cruel as the grave.*
> *Its flashes are flashes of fire,*
> *a most vehement flame.*
> *Many waters cannot quench love,*
> *neither can floods drown it.*
> (8:6, RSV)

In ancient times when few could write, one carried a seal suspended from the neck over the heart or worn on the right hand with which to make his signature — or mark.

In this verse the figure is switched. The woman says to the man — let my name be the seal worn over your heart and on your arm — to say that we belong together, that we are bound together.

From the time young people meet, know each other — to the time they exchange rings and vows in a wedding, they are saying in growing degrees of intensity, "We belong to each other."

We rejoice that John and Susan today say: "We belong to each other. Set me as a seal upon your heart."

The name *Susan* is a Hebrew word meaning *Lily,* one of the most beautiful flowers in the Bible. When in the Song of Songs the man wishes to speak of the unique beauty of his beloved he says: *As a lily among brambles, so is my love among maidens.* And Jesus pointed out the lovely lilies of the field as examples of the Father's world of beauty and trust and faith.

So when you, John, say to Susan, *"You* are as a seal upon my heart," you are saying, *"You* are the loveliest of all to me — a woman of faith and trust."

John is a Hebrew word also — the Father of the brothers Maccabeus, those great strong heroes of ancient Israel who brought independence from Greek tyranny, was John Maccabeus. *John* means *Gift of God.*

When parents name a child, John, they do so because he is God's gift to them. John the Disciple was God's gift to the Church, bringing us the gospel and epistles which remind us *God so loved ... God is love.*

And when you, Susan, say to John, *"You* are as a seal on my heart" you are saying, *"You* are God's gift to me, my strong man — to whom I belong — with whom I shall live and work in this world from this time on!"

A festival of love — such is a marriage — this marriage. We celebrate the strength of love which has brought John and Susan together. We celebrate the staying power of love — so bright a flame nothing can put it out.

And we recognize that the love you have receives its energy and power from that love that never ends, that greatest love of all, the love of God which enfolds us now, and will continue to be with you all the days of your lives together. Amen.

47

Let God Be The Go-Between

By Paul L. Winemiller, Jr.

Text: Mark 10:7-9: *For this reason a man shall leave his father and mother and be joined to his wife, and the two shall become one. So they are no longer two but one. What therefore God has joined together, let no man put asunder.* (RSV)

What are we to believe about marriage today? We certainly read and hear much. Recently a University of Michigan sociologist stated that divorce can be a healthy thing. On a television show, a young husband upon being introduced said, "I have a wonderful wife and a one-year-old daughter, and I love them very much." Truly, marriage and divorce is a controversial subject today. It was also during Jesus' day. And Jesus came up with an observation that goes to the core of the success or failure of marriage: *What therefore God has joined together, let no man put asunder.* Christians did not invent marriage. But Christ has added the following to marriage: God himself takes part in the ceremony. He joins man and woman together to become one. Jesus put marriage between two people on the same unbreakable basis as blood relatives. As we never revoke the tie with the mother and father who raised us, neither should we with the one to whom we are married.

In the Syrian Churches of South India young people meet their lifetime mate through the services of a Go-Between. This Go-Between is a respected person approached by the family or church. The resulting marriages have invariably been happy ones. When asked the reason, couples have responded by saying, "Our marriage is based not on our own feelings but on an act of God."

Today we are asking God's blessing upon the marriage of _____ and _____. We are asking them and you to recognize that it is God who is making them ONE. This does not mean they are giving up their individual characteristics and talents. It means that now they will have the beautiful opportunity of sharing

48

together the talents God has given them. They will also know physical oneness. Not a physical oneness that says our marriage will succeed or fail based on the success of our honeymoon. This gift of God is very important, but it is only one of the bright colors that paint the beautiful picture of marriage. If your marriage is not to *fade* you will need to carefully paint in the colors of constant communication, ready forgiveness, perennial politeness, and a firm faith.

If your marriage is truly to be ONE, let Christ be your constant Go-Between. Take your problems, decisions, and joys to him in prayer. Make the Church a spiritual subdivision of your home by setting up a family altar with daily devotions. Today you are committing yourselves to a lifetime together come what may. It is a big decision. But God helped you make it; he is here blessing you now; and he goes forth with you in the tomorrows if you will but let him.

Jesus knew what he was talking about. You must not take one another for granted. My advice today is simply this: keep Jesus in your plans also. Don't take him for granted! In so far as you keep Christ in your marriage your life together will be an unbroken spiritual oneness until death parts you. May the beautiful picture you are about to paint in the years ahead be of such splendor that everyone who sees you may say, "Truly there is a marriage blessed by God." Amen.

The Beauty Of Marriage

By John M. Braaten

_____ and _____, this is a very special day in
your lives. You have gone to great lengths to make it beautiful.
Now if only there were some way to insure that your marriage
would be beautiful, all the days of your life. I say this, remembering what one wit said, "There's entirely too much worrying about
unhappy marriages. Everyone knows that all marriages are happy.
It's getting along together *after* the marriage that creates the problems."

I think you would agree that almost every marriage begins beautifully; maintaining beauty in the relationship is infinitely more
difficult. However, God has left you neither helpless nor hopeless.
He has a great investment in you both, and his promise is that he
will stand by you to provide you with his mercies, that your marriage might grow in depth and glory.

Saint John writes of how God shares his love with us, but he
also suggests how a marriage can develop an enduring quality of
loveliness: "In this the love of God was made manifest among us,
that God sent his only Son into the world, so that we might live
through him. In this is love, not that we loved God, but that he
loved us and sent his Son to be the expiation for our sins. Beloved,
if God so loved us, we also ought to love one another" (1 John 4:9-
11).

Telling you, or any bride and groom standing before an altar,
that you must love each other sounds as needless as commanding a
three-year-old to eat a candy bar. After all, isn't that what marriage
is all about — love?

The truth is, the kind of love John speaks of is far different
from what people usually mean when they talk of love. Love is
most often regarded as a romantic feeling, but for John, love is far
deeper, more beautiful, and more consuming. John's love is not an
emotion; it is an event. He refers to the kind of love God has for us.

When God wanted to reveal his love to us in its most awesome wonder, he permitted his Son, Jesus, to be crucified. In the crucified Christ, God showed us he was willing to go further than anyone could be asked, in order to prove his love. It was on Calvary that God in Christ redefined love for us. God was saying that love is forgiveness; love is reconciliation; love is restoring, healing, helping; therein is love!

And so, _____ and _____, when John tells you to love one another, he is not saying something that is patently obvious. In reality he is saying nothing less than this: you are both dearly loved by God. Now he has given each of you the responsibility of bearing that sacrificial kind of love into your relationship. In other words, God's love and grace take human form as you care for and share with each other. That means the love you are to foster in your marriage is not simply a feeling, no matter how warm and affectionate, but an action. God's kind of love is always at work. It is not so much a noun as it is a verb. It is a love which works toward harmony and fulfillment. It is a love which grows out of the emotions of courtship to create charitable acts of compassion and kindness.

_____ and _____, love will be evident in your marriage when you forgive one another. Love will be illustrated when there is healing and encouragement. Love will be practiced when you help each other and support one another. A love that works to help, heal, restore, and forgive, can make your marriage beautiful — exquisitely beautiful — not only for yourselves, but for all who are in your company.

Love is an event first demonstrated for us by our Lord who gave himself for us. Now he invites you, _____ and _____, to continue that self-giving love in your married life. It will not always be easy. The love which is in the shape of forgiveness will need to be practiced often; there is no other way for you to be truly happy.

And remember, the God who created the institution of marriage is as near as your thoughts. Through devotions, prayers, and regular worship he can constantly remind you of his burning love. Through the Holy Spirit he can give you the mind of Christ, which

51

will soften your wills so God's kind of self-sacrificing love can become active in your lives. For only the love which is an event — the love that heals, forgives, strengthens, and restores — abides forever. Love which is active can make your marriage a thing of beauty from beginning to end.

We celebrate this day, this day of love, for today you are brought together and united in an atmosphere of charm and beauty. Our prayers will follow you, that living in God's glorious grace you may find your marriage growing in beauty as the years pass by. Amen.

Grow Not In Each Other's Shadow

By Leslie F. Brandt

In his book *The Prophet*, Kahlil Gibran talks about marriage:

> *You were born together, and together you shall be forevermore.*
> *You shall be together when the white wings of death scatter your days.*
> *Aye, you shall be together even in the silent memory of God.*
> *But let there be spaces in your togetherness.,*
> *And let the winds of the heavens dance between you.*
> *Love one another but make not a bond of love;*
> *Let it rather be a moving sea between the shores of your souls.*
> *Fill each other's cup but drink not from one cup.*
> *Give one another of your bread but eat not from the same loaf.*
> *Sing and dance together and be joyous, but let each one of you be alone,*
> *Even as the strings of a lute are alone though they quiver with the same music.*
> *Give your hearts, but not into each other's keeping.*
> *For only the hand of Life can contain your hearts.*
> *And stand together yet not too near together:*
> *For the pillars of the temple stand apart,*
> *And the oak tree and the cypress grow not in each other's shadow.*[1]

I think this author says something very important that we need to hear and to consider. In past years, marriage has often been considered some kind of a contract whereby man and woman own each other and possess each other. It is this very treatment of marriage by so many that has endangered it or destroyed it for them, or has turned it into a kind of cage that thwarts or imprisons the individual personality of one or both within the marital relationship.

We are to disclose ourselves, give of ourselves to the other, but we surrender our total beings only into the possession of God. God only has the right to total possession of our individual beings. Respect the other's individuality; love the other as he or she is; help the other to be a total person. Your relationship will then be a healthy and contributive relationship that will bless each of you and will serve God and fellowman.

---

1. Kahlil Gibran, *The Prophet* (New York: Alfred A. Knopf, 1969), pp. 16-17.

A Motto For Marriage

By Duane T. Wuggazer

You have come here this evening to be joined together in holy matrimony. You have been looking forward to this day with eager and joyful hearts. For months you have been making plans and preparations, and now that long expected hour, where your love is to be crowned with the blessings of God's church, is upon you.

It is a very important moment in life when two young people, who were once strangers to one another, are drawn together by an irresistible attraction, so that their souls cannot be separated by time and space. From this moment on, you are going to live together as husband and wife, for better or worse. From now on you will not be able to hide your various moods or feelings. The fullest impact of your personalities and natures will be brought to bear upon each other.

There is no denying that *faults* are going to appear in one another that up to this point have been hidden in a golden mist. There will be times when all the good qualities that you now see in one another may seem to fade.

But with all of this you should remain unmoved in your devotion and loyalty to one another.

If you want your marriage to be touched with perennial beauty, then you ought to cherish the sound advice given by him who first founded this institution. He has given us certain rules and regulations by which we are to live our lives. These rules and regulations are found in his book, the Holy Bible. They are given to serve as the rudder of the ship of your life.

*The *couple* who commence their married life in the Savior's name; the *man* who knows that he, even as Christ loved the church, should love his wife; the *woman* who knows that Jesus wants her to be a helpmeet to her husband, such people can be very sure they have built their home on a solid foundation.

Further, a *home* this is established with Jesus as the third member of the household; the *fireside*, where a deep sense of devotion to the Word of God pervades the atmosphere, is going to be a dwelling place of contentment and joy, and one which will raise your sights above the commonplace experiences of life.

If you are willing to make real this ideal in your united lives ... if you are willing to place each day of your life in the hands of your Savior for guidance and strength, then I can assure you that the Son of God's grace will never cease to shine over your new home.

(I have on occasion used the following as an alternate conclusion beginning at the *.)

If you take each day of your life and place it into the hands of your Savior for guidance and direction, your home will be a dwelling place of contentment and joy.

You should resolve, with God's help, that your love will not be blotted out nor blurred by the commonplace experiences of life.

It is the prayer of all of us here this evening — your parents, your relatives and your friends — that God may keep his hand over you as in a perpetual benediction, and that he may make your home everything that both he and you want it to be.

I would like to suggest, then, this beautiful motto for you to place over the door of your new home:

> *Then here will I and mine today*
> *A solemn covenant make and say:*
> *Though all the world forsake thy word*
> *I and my house will serve the Lord.*

Christian Marriage

By Elmer E. Flack

(Meditation delivered at the marriage of the author's elder grandson)

Text: Romans 15:5-6: "May the God of steadfastness and encouragement grant you to live in such harmony with one another, in accord with Christ Jesus, that together you may with one voice glorify the God and Father of our Lord Jesus Christ." (RSV)

This prayer of the apostle Paul seems very appropriate for this special occasion when a prospective minister of the gospel takes a mate for the manse. It suggests several thoughts.

1. Marriage is a gift of God. "Unless the Lord build the house, those who build it labor in vain." It is God who sets the solitary in families. "Therefore a man leaves his father and his mother and cleaves to his wife, and they become one flesh." The family is the oldest social institution on earth. Luther called the family "the little church."

2. God desires harmony in marriage. God is a God of patience and consolation, of steadfastness and encouragement, who gives to husband and wife the grace to be likeminded, to live in harmony with one another, to share with each other the totality of life's experiences. His blessing makes for mutual accord. *An Gottes Segen ist alles gelegen!*

3. Christian marriage is a spiritual union. This is a great mystery, likened unto the union of Christ and his Church. Just as Christ loved the Church, so ought husbands to love their wives; and likewise wives, their husbands. This union in marriage is not primarily civic, nor physical, nor social, nor economic, but spiritual. In this union in accord with Christ love finds expression in mutual submission, forbearance, patience, kindness, respect, fidelity, and sacrificial suffering. Christ molds marriage into a garden of grace. The highest experience of single bliss and blessedness in no way transcends the holiness of Christian matrimony.

4. Christian marriage glorifies God. Paul prays that "together you may with one voice glorify the God and Father of our Lord Jesus Christ." Modeled after Christ's union with his Bride, the Church, Christian marriage bears witness to God's grace in Christ. The true Christian home is where "Christ is the Head of the house, the unseen Guest at every meal, and the silent Listener to every conversation." Such a home is a vestibule of heaven as well as a bulwark of the nation. It bears witness to the world how sublime and unselfish, how pure and holy, how tender and true Christian family love can be.

And when this home becomes a manse, the home of a minister of the gospel, it can stand as a mansion of Christian testimony, a model of true love. The minister's home does well to set the life pattern of witnessing for Christ with heart and voice, with word and deed, in mutual forbearance, forgiveness, fidelity, and love. We pray that this union now to be consummated with the holy vows may be in Christ such a model home consecrated for his service.

Paul's prayer is our prayer today: "May the God of steadfastness and encouragement grant you to live in such harmony with one another, in accord with Christ Jesus, that *together* you may with one voice glorify the God and Father of our Lord Jesus Christ." Amen.

Hope In Christ

By Elmer E. Flack

(Meditation delivered at the marriage of the author's younger grandson)

Grace to you and peace from God our Father and our Lord Jesus Christ. Amen.

Text: Romans 12:12: "Rejoice in your hope, be patient in tribulation, be constant in prayer." (RSV)

It seems particularly appropriate to base this marriage meditation upon the text which the groom's great-grandfather, the Reverend Hugo J. Dorow, D.D., employed fifty years ago at the marriage of his grandfather and grandmother, who last week celebrated their Golden Wedding Anniversary. We wish to cite the text in Phillip's translation: "Base your happiness on your hope in Christ. When trials come endure them patiently; steadfastly maintain the habit of prayer."

1. Base your happiness on your hope in Christ. Here is the real secret of a happy marriage. A home cannot be built with solidity, serenity, and satisfaction on any other foundation than that which is laid in Christ. Foundations of "gold, silver, precious stones, wood ..." or whatever the material basis are insecure. They lack the strength and support of the Rock of Ages.

Every couple entering the bonds of holy matrimony cherishes the hope of a happy married life. But on every hand we observe in the midst of the complexities of our modern world the plight of innumerable unhappy and broken homes, homes resting upon improper foundations and false standards of family life.

But the home in which the husband loves his wife as Christ also loved the Church and gave himself for it, and in which the wife likewise loves and cherishes her mate is such as has an anchor of hope that insures continuing happiness. As you now enter this holy estate be sure to base your happiness on your hope in Christ.

2. When trials come, endure them patiently. Although by reason of sin, many a cross is laid thereon, nevertheless our gracious Father in heaven does not forsake his children in an estate so holy and acceptable to him.

However severe the vicissitudes, however heavy the burdens to be borne in the building and maintenance of home and family life through sickness, suffering, and sorrow, as well as through days of prosperity, peace, and pleasure, patient endurance with faith firmly fixed on Christ who suffered for us may always find the way to meet life's demands. Christ teaches us how to face hardships and adversity as also how gratefully to receive the measures of his love and grace. When your trials come, endure them patiently.

3. Steadfastly maintain the habit of prayer. Personal and family devotions faithfully followed day by day open wide the gates of grace and permit the blessings of heaven to flow freely upon a home and family thus habituated. Families that pray together stay together.

This threefold formula will insure for you as it has for grandparents over a half century a very happy and blessed marriage: hope in Christ, patient endurance of trials, and persistence in prayer. May God bless abundantly your lives together! Amen.

Living In Harmony

By Elmer E. Flack

(Meditation delivered at the marriage of the author's grand-daughter)

Text: Philippians 2:1ff: "Now if your experience of Christ's encouragement and love means anything to you, if you have known something of the fellowship of his Spirit, and all that it means in kindness and deep sympathy, do make my best hopes for you come true! Live together in harmony, live together in love, as though you had only one mind and one spirit between you." (Phillips)

1. True love stems from Christ. In his love letter to the Philippians Paul writes: "If your experience of Christ's encouragement and love means anything to you ...." And I am sure that it does. You have been brought together in Christian faith and encouragement to know the love of Christ. Says Paul, "The love of Christ controls us," or "constrains us." It restrains us from the pursuit of our own selfish ways, controls our actions, and directs us in ways of truth, uprightness, forbearance, and understanding. "The very spring of our actions is the love of Christ," as Phillips renders it.

2. This love is directed by his Spirit. "If you have known something of the fellowship of his Spirit," says Paul. The Holy Spirit is our true marriage counselor, guide, and comforter, who knits together human hearts in love and fellowship. Paul is certain that by the operation of God's Spirit through the Means of Grace you will come to know what all this "means in kindness and deep sympathy." Participation in the Spirit makes for true love and affection. For such are the fruits of the Spirit — love, joy, peace, patience, kindness, goodness, faithfulness, gentleness, self-control." It is Christ who by his Spirit blesses the home with harmony, love, and unity.

61

3. This love accepts counsel. Recognizing then the source of our love and devotion, let us receive with thankfulness Paul's advice and counsel:

"Live together in harmony." Many homes today are out of harmony because they are out of touch with Christ and his Church. In and by the aid of the Spirit a couple can live together in harmony and mutual understanding. Harmony in marriage means working together in full accord, with full recognition of rights, respect, esteem, and encouragement; having common ardor, common purpose, common interests, sharing all assets, all confidences, all longings, all desires. It means living together, praying together, worshiping together, rejoicing together, sorrowing together when sorrow comes. Happy the home where harmony reigns!

"Live together in love." This goes even deeper. It involves all our thoughts and actions. True love adorns the whole family life with devotion, affection, beauty, and blessing. It involves kindness, sympathy, forgiveness, forbearance, thoughtfulness of the needs of another, and willingness to sacrifice and serve in joy and sorrow, in sickness and in health.

"Live together ... as though you had only one mind and one spirit between you." Marriage is a great mystery. It is inexplicable how two people are really made one. But such is the scriptural account of God's action in creating the home: "Therefore a man leaves his father and his mother and cleaves to his wife, and they become one flesh." This unity is God's creation. Hence the scriptural injunction: "What God has joined together, let not man put asunder." Whatever disturbs this harmony and unity disturbs all society, parents, children, relatives, neighbors, friends, and associates. Whatever promotes this unity serves to preserve the integrity, the sanctity, and the strength not only of the home and family life but also of the web and woof of all human society. May your home be a home of harmony, love, and true Christian unity!

We conclude with Paul: "Let this mind be in you which was also in Christ Jesus."

The Greatest Of These Is Love

By Kenneth H. Sauer

(A wedding homily for the service of marriage for two people who had been previously married)

Text: 1 Corinthians 13:13: So faith, hope, love abide, these three: but the greatest of these is love. (RSV)

This is one of those powerful verses in the Bible that we could never forget. Paul is here culminating his argument for the dynamic of Christian living.

It is not a wistful dream that the past will be overcome and forgotten that gives motivation for life. It is not a blind expectation that the future will work out all right that gives courage for living. It is the present experience of love that gives assurance that the past is meaningful, and the future is filled with promise.

The love of which Paul speaks is love of man for man, man for woman, parents for children. But it is love which has its source and beginning in God's love for us.

We love because he first loved us. We can love because we know his love in Jesus Christ. We experience now the power of acceptance and concern that God has for us.

You experience **now** the affection and concerns for each other. **What** you know now enable you to take your past up in faith that it was as preparation for this day, and to look with joy to the future in **hope.**

The **love of God** has come to you both; you know him; you trust his Word. **Love** has come between you both as you have come to care for one another.

Out of the power of this present reality you can look at the future with a vibrant joy, for before you are fruitful years of gladness.

So faith, hope, love abide ... these three; but the greatest of these is love. See what love the Father has given us, that we should be called children of God; and so we are.

On this happy day for you, this **love of God** will deepen your love for each other and with you **faith** and **hope** will abide; but the greatest of these is love. Amen.

Self-Disclosure — Self-Surrender

By Leslie F. Brandt

In a world where good interpersonal relationships are hard to come by, marriage, potentially the most effective kind of relationship, can also be the most destructive one. After counseling with scores of frustrated spouses on the brink of breakup, one begins to focus on keys or clues to a reasonably happy and lasting relationship. Wise budgeting and good sexual techniques are important. Common interests between mates certainly makes a contribution. Communication and motivation are vital to the cause. But two key phrases that deserve priority in a successful relationship are first, self-disclosure, and secondly, self-surrender.

First, there must be self-disclosure — to each other. We are all guilty of assuming roles in our lives — playing games with each other. Suspicious and ashamed of our real selves, we take on one or more of the roles acquired, often unconsciously, from our parents or teachers or some other authority figure in our lives. Thus we parade around under masks, not daring to expose our real selves for fear of rejection or nonacceptance by our mates. Before one can truly love another, he must disclose himself to the other. Before one can disclose himself, he must accept himself as valid and worthwhile. Then he must honestly BE himself, reveal himself, give of himself.

Then, there must be self-surrender — to God. In a paraphrase of Psalm 61, the psalmist prays: "I cannot find peace or security until I lose myself in something or someone that is greater than I." We don't surrender ourselves to each other. We disclose ourselves, give of ourselves to the other, but we surrender our all to God. God only has the right to total possession of our beings. "So faith, hope, love abide, these three: but the greatest of these is love." It is to love — as manifested through Jesus Christ — that I commend you.

Mystical And Real

By Paul O. Hamsher

(This wedding meditation was used at the marriage of a young couple in the author's parish. The service included the hymn, "O Perfect Love" and Psalm 128, with the guests participating. The wedding party took their places in the front pew following the processional and remained there until after the meditation.)

"Marriage is a holy estate, ordained of God, and to be held in honor by all." We hear these words in every marriage ceremony; that is, if the wedding is held in a Christian church. They are words which hold the key to understanding the difference between a civil ceremony and a church wedding. But what do these words mean?

There is the obvious answer, of course, that God instituted marriage in order to propagate the race. The family institution was necessary for the protection of children through their long years of preparation for adulthood. To insure a proper environment for growth and learning, to provide a channel for passing on from generation to generation all the accumulated heritage of humankind, God ordained marriage as a holy estate to be held in honor by all.

But let's look a little deeper. God made man in his own image. That is, he gave to man something of his own attributes. He made man a thinking animal. He gave man the power to reason, the power to imagine, invent and create. And above all, he gave man the power to love. God *is* Love. When he made man in his own image he gave him this supreme divine attribute. Yes, love is the greatest. It is what draws two people together. It is the power that unites a man and a woman to make them one.

Let's make no mistake at this point. The love we are talking about is far more than infatuation. It goes way beyond mere physical attraction. It is the sharing with one another the greatest attribute of God. The recognition of this fact is the true secret of happiness in marriage.

Does this sound too mystical? Do you think I'm not being very realistic? Well, look at the facts. You are a young couple in love, happy in the prospect of establishing a new Christian home. You want this happiness to go on forever. But let's face it. You are not going to have this happiness always. The first romance will fade. Monotony will set in. There will be wearisome, dull days. There may be times when you think that all there is to living is making a living. You may think at times that this was all a big mistake. There will be crises to face, perhaps even tragedies. What then?

You see, I am being very realistic now. And I am saying that by acknowledging the fact that marriage is the sharing with one another the greatest attribute of God, your love will be big enough and strong enough to carry you through anything and everything life holds for you.

There is no such thing as a perfect marriage, for the simple reason that every marriage is the union of two imperfect human beings. But there is a third factor for you. You are beginning your marriage with God. Continue to include him, every day, remembering that God is Love. You will grow together toward the ideal. This will be the source of your real happiness, a happiness that nothing can take from you — ever.

Love, Honor, Forgive

By Leslie F. Brandt

If you had been married forty years ago, you might have subscribed to the vows to "love, honor, and obey ..." your mate or spouse. We put an end to that, but maybe we should substitute an alternate and ask of each of you to "love, honor, and forgive."

It is interesting to speculate on how much our divorce rates could be cut down if "forgiveness" were as much a part of the marital relationship as, for instance, the conjugal bed. Divorce might even be outmoded — or at least reserved for deeply serious cases of incompatibility or negligence.

The word "love" in our day refers to almost everything from apple pie to sexual orgies. Whatever its true and accurate meaning, it certainly must include the ability and willingness to forgive. We could not conceive of divine love apart from forgiveness. Human love, which is essentially a reflection of divine love, is not really love at all unless it is a forgiving love. We may be full of poetry and music toward our mates as long as their affections and activities pamper our egos, but this can hardly be construed as love.

We must "love, honor, and forgive." This must begin with our acceptance of God's incomprehensible love and forgiveness. It must be followed, and this is inculcated in such acceptance, by our ability to forgive ourselves. A humble and honest appraisal of ourselves should certainly make us tender, acceptive, understanding, forgiving toward our mate or fellowman. It does not mean that we must condone our own. But we may have to learn how to tolerate the weaknesses he or she has not yet learned how to transform into strength, the liabilities he or she has not yet turned into assets. We need to accept each other as valid, significant, worthwhile persons, even in the midst of or including our failure-fraught flesh.

"Love, honor, and forgive." It is essential to happy and effective marital and interpersonal relationships. It is possible only by the grace of God. It is to that grace that I now commend you.

Service For The Fiftieth Anniversary

By Michael B. Goldner
Wesley T. Runk

Order Of Service

Organ Prelude Music

"Sinfonia"	J.S. Bach
"Thanks Be To Thee"	George F. Handel
"Jesu, Joy Of Man's Desiring"	J.S. Bach
"Psalm XVIII"	Benedetto Marcello
	arranged by Denes Agay
Organ Chimes	"O Perfect Love"

Congregational Hymn   "Holy, Holy, Holy"
(Congregation standing)

The Invocation *(Read responsively)*
P: In the name of the Father, and of the Son, and of the Holy Ghost.
Amen.
O Lord, open thou my lips.
C: **And my mouth shall show forth thy praise.**
P: Make haste, O God, to deliver me.
C: **Make haste to help me, O Lord.**
P: Glory be to the Father, and to the Son, and to the Holy Ghost;
C: **As it was in the beginning, is now, and ever shall be world
without end. Amen**

Psalm No. 128 *(Read responsively)*
P: Blessed is every one that feareth the Lord;
C: **That walketh in his ways.**
P: For thou shalt eat the labor of thine hands.
C: **Happy shalt thou be, and it shall be well with thee.**
P: Thy wife shall be as a fruitful vine by the sides of thine house:

C: **Thy children like olive plants round about thy table.**
P: Behold, that thus shall the man be blessed:
C: **That feareth the Lord.**
P: The Lord shall bless thee out of Zion:
C: **And thou shalt see the good of Jerusalem all the days of thy life.**
P: Yea, thou shalt see thy children's children.
C: **And peace upon Israel.**

(Congregation seated)

The Covenant Of The Marriage Vows

The grace of the Lord Jesus Christ, the love of the Father, and the fellowship of the Spirit be with you. Amen.

In this place shall be heard once again the sounds of joy and gladness. Happy are all who fear the Lord, who live according to his will.

It is fitting on such an occasion as this, that we recall with reverent minds, what the Word of God teacheth concerning the Holy Estate of Marriage.

The apostle Paul, speaking by the Holy Spirit said: Husbands, love your wives, even as Christ also loved the Church, and gave himself for it. He that loveth his wife, loveth himself; for no man ever yet hated his own flesh, but nourisheth it, even as the Lord, the Church. Wives, submit yourselves unto your own husbands, as unto the Lord; for the husband is the head of the wife, even as Christ is the Head of the Church.

And although, by reason of sin, many a cross hath been laid thereon, nevertheless our gracious Father in heaven doth not forsake his children in an estate so holy and acceptable to him, but is ever present with his abundant blessing.

The Scripture Lesson   The Wedding at Cana
                                               John 2:1-11

Congregational Hymn   "Breathe On Me, Breath Of God"

70

Words Of Celebration

Let us pray in unison. *(Kneeling)*

Father of love, shower your grace upon these thy children, who have come this day to worship and give thanks for their fifty years of life together. Grant them the strength and patience, the affection and understanding, the courage and love to continue together in mutual growth according to thy will.

May each of us be reminded of our covenant with thee, to live our lives in faith and fidelity. As thou hast made covenant with thy Holy Church, so also bless and guard the lives of all who have assembled this day, until thou hast accomplished thy purposes through them.

This we pray in the Name of Jesus our Lord, who taught us when we pray to say ...

Our Father, who art in Heaven ... (The Lord's Prayer)

Congregational Hymn   "On Our Way Rejoicing"

(Congregation standing)

The Benediction

Organ Chimes   "A Mighty Fortress"

Silent Prayer

Postlude   "Joyful, Joyful We Adore Thee"
Arr. by Richard Ellsasser